The material was previously published in the book *The Big Book of Socks: The Ultimate Beyond-the-Basics Guide to Knitting Socks* (ISBN 978-1-60085-085-1)
First published in this format 2012

The Taunton Press, Inc., 63 South Main Street, PO Box 5506, Newtown, CT 06470-5506
e-mail: tp@taunton.com

Interior Design and Layout: L49 Design
Illustrator: Christine Erikson
Photographers: Burcu Avsar and Zach DeSart

Printed in the United States of America
10 9 8 7 6 5 4 3 2 1

Table of Contents

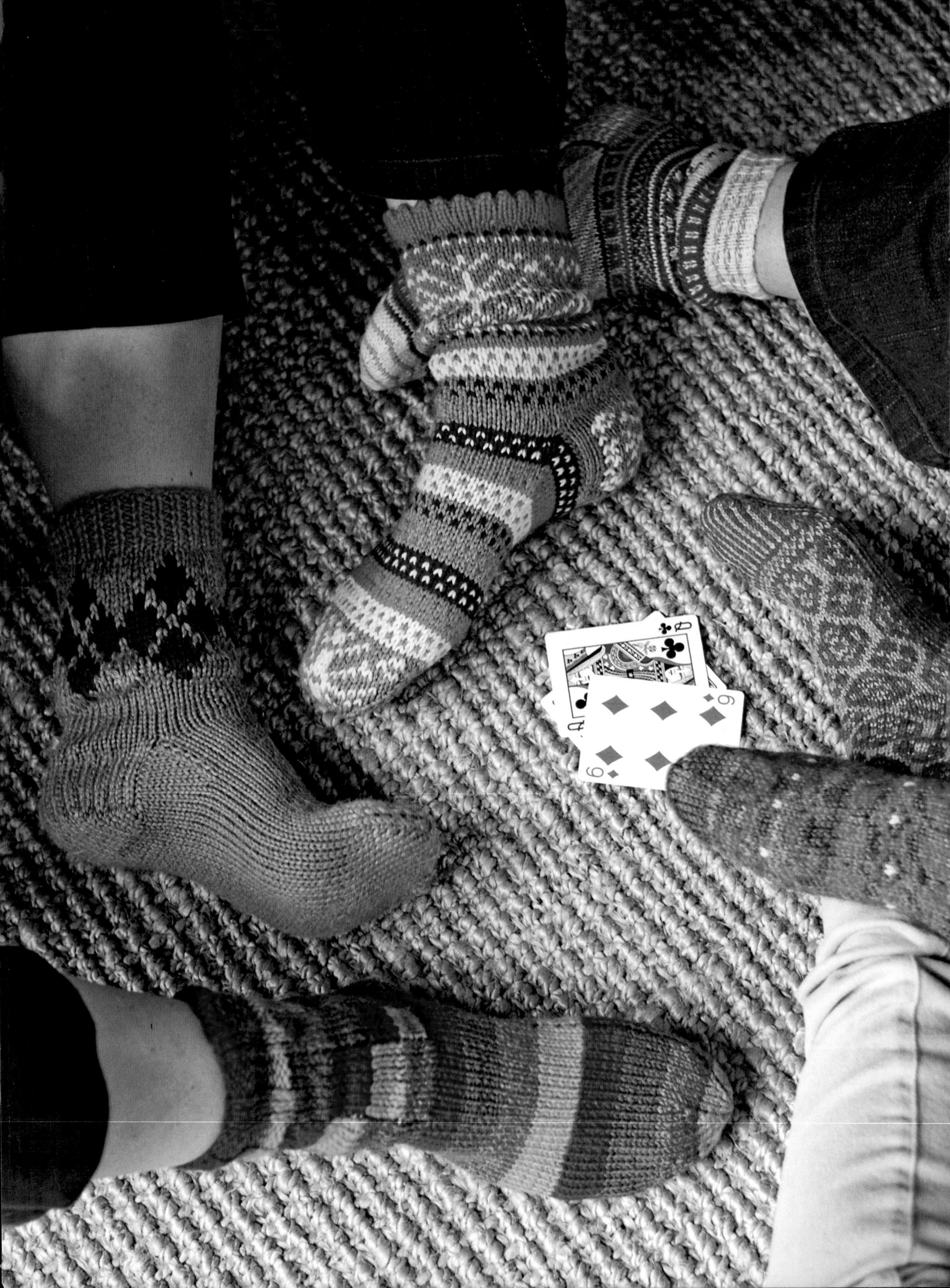

Colorwork

Colorwork is just knitting with more than one color. To carry the different yarns, I hold strands with my right hand, then pick up the color I need with the left needle. Others hold a strand in each hand. The important thing is to strand the unused yarn loosely from section to section.

It's important, too, to take color *dominance* into consideration with stranded knitting. Whether you hold both of your strands in one hand, or one in each hand, always hold and strand the motif color underneath the background color. That will cause your motif color to dominate the background color. If you're knitting a sock with many color changes, decide for each border which color will be dominant. If you're knitting socks with just two colors, such as our Mosaic Tile Sock, decide which color will be dominant and maintain that dominance consistently throughout, unless you want your socks to have very different looking stripes.

Intarsia knitting is often worked flat and involves using many colors per row, holding one strand at a time and switching colors (by twisting the strands around each other) at new sections. Each colored area of an intarsia design is worked with a separate length of yarn. Those lengths can be wound on cardboard bobbins. In all cases, you do colorwork by reading a chart (I like to make a color copy) that indicates which stitches to work in which colors.

Stripes and Stairsteps SOCK

This intermediate pattern, sized to fit children through adults, is a good introduction to intarsia work because it uses fairly short yarn lengths for the stairstep blocks. Just let the yarns hang free from the back of your needle instead of winding them on bobbins (shown at left in Knit Picks Telemark™).

PATTERN DIFFICULTY: Intermediate
YARN: Fine Weight Yarn (CYCA 2), approx. 100 (100, 100, 200, 200) yd. each of Burgundy, Green, Purple, and Yellow
YARN WEIGHT: Fine (CYCA 2)
NEEDLES: Size 4 (U.S.)/3.5 mm, or size needed to obtain gauge 10-in. straight or circular, as desired
TOOLS: Large-eye blunt needle, stitch markers
PATTERN SIZES: Child (10–11, 12–13), Youth (1–2, 3–4), Women's Average (5–6, 7–8, 9–10), Men's Average, Men's Wide (8–9, 10–11, 12–13)
MEASUREMENTS: Cuff Length: Child: 4 in., Youth: 5 in., Women's: 6 in., Men's: 7 in.; Cuff Width, Unsewn: Child: 5½ in., Youth: 6½ in., Women's Average: 7⅜ in., Men's Average: 8⅜ in., Men's Wide: 9⅜ in.; Heel-to-Toe Length: Child Shoe Size 10–11: 5½ in., Child Shoe Size 12–13: 6¼ in., Youth Shoe Size 1–2: 7 in., Youth Shoe Size 3–4: 7½ in., Women's Shoe Size 5–6: 9 in., Women's Shoe Size 7–8: 9½ in., Women's Shoe Size 9–10: 10 in., Men's Shoe Size 8–9: 10½ in., Men's Shoe Size 10–11: 11 in., Men's Shoe Size 12–13: 12 in.
HEEL STYLE: Two-Needle Afterthought
GAUGE: 6.5 sts = 1 in., 8 rows = 1 in. in Stockinette st

It takes approximately 42 in. of yarn to knit each individual intarsia square on this pattern. You may wind the loose yarn on bobbins, or you may leave the ends hanging. Tie on new colors as indicated on the chart, leaving at least a 3-in. tail. When changing colors, wrap the new color around the old color on the wrong side of the work before continuing.

Note: If you want your socks to be mirror images of each other, knit the right sock as directed. Knit the left sock by beginning at the opposite side of the chart.

Note: Work **Women's Wide** as for **Men's Average**; adjust length for shoe size. Work **Women's Narrow** as for **Youth**; adjust length for shoe size.

RIGHT SOCK With size 4 straight or circular needle and Burgundy, CO 36 (42, 48, 54, 60) sts.

Work 4 rows in K3, P3 ribbing, working back and forth. Cut Burgundy and tie on Green, and work 4 rows in K3, P3 ribbing. Rep with Purple and Yellow.

FIRST CUFF RND: With Yellow, P across. Turn.

Follow chart as indicated, beginning all sizes except Men's Average at the right upper corner of the chart. Begin Men's Average at the right upper corner of the chart, on the stitch indicated. Continue, repeating chart as needed, until cuff measures 4 in. (5 in., 6 in., 7 in., 7 in.). End with WS row at the bottom of a square.

RIGHT HEEL DIVISION ROW 1: With Burgundy, BO 18 (21, 24, 27, 30) sts, K remainder of row.

RIGHT HEEL DIVISION ROW 2: P 18 (21, 24, 27, 30) sts, CO 18 (21, 24, 27, 30) sts.

Continue working foot on 36 (42, 48, 54, 60) sts in Stockinette st, in 8-row stripes of Burgundy, Green, Purple, Yellow, repeating the stripe sequence if necessary, until foot measures: Child Shoe Size 10–11: 2½ in., Child Shoe Size 12–13: 4 in., Youth Shoe Size 1–2: 4½ in., Youth Shoe Size 3–4: 4¾ in., Women's Shoe Size 5–6: 5½ in., Women's Shoe Size 7–8: 6 in., Women's Shoe Size 9–10: 6½ in., Men's Shoe Size 8–9: 6½ in., Men's Shoe Size 10–12: 7 in., Men's Shoe Size 13: 7 in. End with a P row.

TOE Continuing in established stripe sequence, work a 36 (42, 48, 54, 60)-st Star Toe as instructed on page 177. Cut a 12-in. tail, and thread the yarn through a large-eye needle. Thread the needle through the remaining loops, tighten, and tie off. Do not weave loose end in.

LEFT SOCK Work ribbing and cuff as for Right Sock, end with a **Knit** row.

LEFT HEEL DIVISION ROW 1 (WS): BO 18 (21, 24, 27, 30) sts, **Purl** rem of row.

LEFT HEEL DIVISION ROW 2: **Knit** 18 (21, 24, 27, 30) sts, CO 18 (21, 24, 27, 30) sts.

Complete foot as for Right Sock.

Note: Work heel in 4-row stripes in the following order: Burgundy, Green, Purple, Yellow. Rep sequence if necessary.

BOTH SOCKS **AFTERTHOUGHT HEEL ROW 1:** With Burgundy, on the WS of the sock, pick up and P 18 (21, 24, 27, 30) sts along one edge of the heel opening, place marker, along the other edge of the heel opening, pick up and P 18 (21, 24, 27, 30) sts. (36, 42, 48, 54, 60 sts)

AFTERTHOUGHT HEEL ROW 2: SSK, K to within 2 sts of the marker, K2 tog, move marker, SSK, K to within 2 sts of the end of the row, K2 tog. (4 sts dec)

AFTERTHOUGHT HEEL ROW 3: P.

Rep Rows 2–3 until there are 16 (22, 24, 26, 30) sts left. Divide the rem sts on 2 needles so that the decs are at the beginning and the end of each needle. You may need to work half of the sts so that the yarn is at the working end of the needle. Close the heel with Kitchener st (see Glossary for instructions). Tighten and tie off.

FINISHING Line up the heel side seam and sew it with yarn threaded in a large-eye needle, using the Mattress st (see Glossary for instructions). Sew the sock side seam, lining up squares on the cuff and stripes on the foot. Tie off ends, and weave all loose ends in on the inside of the sock. Wash and block the socks.

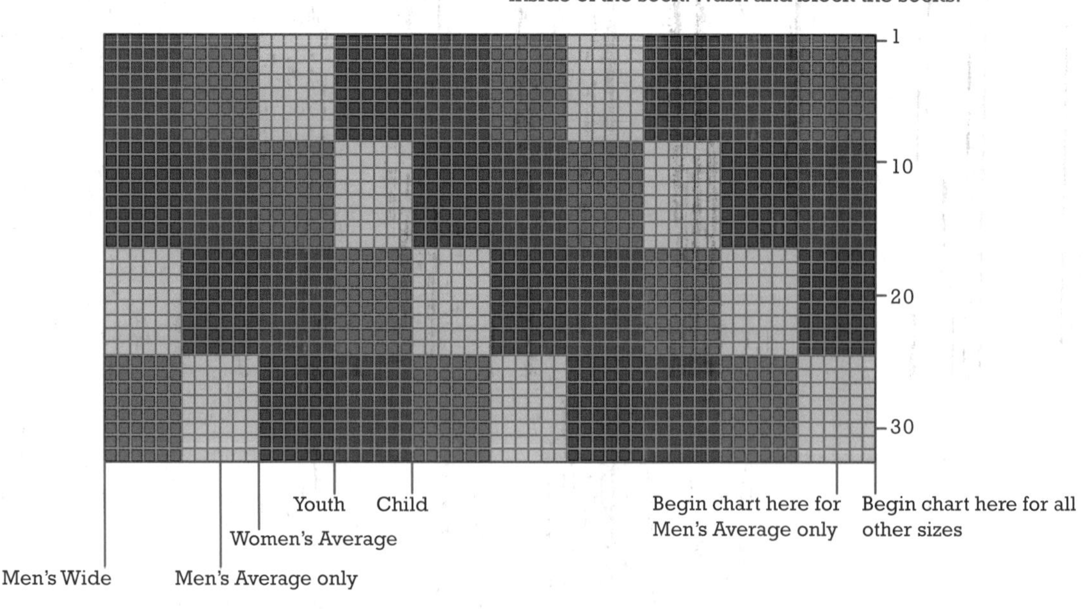

STRIPES AND STAIRSTEPS INTARSIA CHART

Argyle BORDER SOCK

Argyle styling and luxury yarns combine to make this classic sock a keeper. Knit the cuff flat, and then join and knit the heel and foot in the round (shown on page 9 knit in Knit Picks Andean Silk).

PATTERN DIFFICULTY: Intermediate

YARN: Medium Weight Yarn (CYCA 4), approx. 200 (200, 300) yd. Green; 100 (200, 200) yd. Tan; 100 yd. Blue

YARN WEIGHT: Medium (CYCA 4)

NEEDLES: 1 pair 10-in. straight size 5 (U.S.)/3.75 mm needles, or size needed to obtain gauge
1 or 2 circular needles or 4 or 5 dpns, as desired

TOOLS: Large-eye blunt needle, stitch markers

PATTERN SIZES: Youth (1–2, 3–4), Women's (5–6, 7–8, 9–10), Men's (8–9, 10–11, 12–13)

MEASUREMENTS: Cuff Length: Youth: 6 in., Women's: 6½ in., Men's: 7 in.; Cuff Width: Youth: 3¼ in., Women's: 4 in., Men's: 5 in.; Foot Width: Youth: 3¼ in., Women's: 3¾ in., Men's: 4¾ in.; Heel-to-Toe Length: Youth Shoe Size 1–2: 6½ in., Youth Shoe Size 3–4: 7 in., Women's Shoe Size 5–6: 8½ in., Women's Shoe Size 7–8: 9 in., Women's Shoe Size 9–10: 10 in., Men's Shoe Size 8–9: 10 in., Men's Shoe Size 10–11: 11 in., Men's Shoe Size 12–13: 12 in.

HEEL STYLE: Flap and Gusset

GAUGE: 6.5 sts = 1 in., 8 rnds = 1 in. in Stockinette st
6 sts = 1 in., 8 rows = 1 in. over Argyle Pattern

Note: Tie on a new strand of yarn for each color section. You may wind the loose yarn on bobbins, or you may leave the ends hanging (this yarn is slick and doesn't tangle easily). Tie on new colors as indicated on the chart, leaving at least a 3-in. tail. When changing colors, wrap the new color around the old color on the wrong side of the work before continuing.

Note: Work **Women's Narrow** as for **Youth**; adjust cuff and foot length for shoe size.

With Tan and size 5 straight needles, CO 40 (50, 60) sts.

Work K1, P1 ribbing for 12 (15, 20) rows. End with RS row.

CUFF SETUP (WS) P across.

CUFF Beginning at Row 1 as indicated, work the chart, end with a WS row.

NEXT ROW: K with Green.

NEXT ROW: P with Green.

Transfer sts to 1 or 2 circulars or 3 or 4 dpns, as desired, with the center back cuff opening the beginning of the new rnd.

RND 1, YOUTH: Inc 2 sts evenly spaced in rnd. (42 sts)

RND 1, WOMEN'S: Dec 2 sts evenly spaced in rnd. (48 sts)

RND 1, MEN'S: K. (60 sts)

Work even in Green until cuff measures 6 in. (6½ in., 7 in.).

HEEL SETUP K 10 (12, 15) sts. Place the next 22 (24, 30) sts on a separate needle or holder for the instep. Place the rem 10 (12, 15) sts with the first for the heel. (20, 24, 30 heel sts)

HEEL FLAP ROW 1: Cut Green. Tie on Tan. Turn. Sl 1, P across. Turn.

HEEL FLAP ROW 2: *Sl 1, K 1*, rep across. Turn.

Rep Heel Flap Rows 1–2 until heel flap measures 1½ in. (2 in., 2½ in.). End with a P row.

HEEL Work a 20 (24, 30)-st Flap and Gusset Heel as instructed on pages 172–173.

GUSSET SETUP Sl 1, K5 (6, 8). Cut Tan.
Tie on Green.

GUSSET RND 1: K6 (7, 9), pick up, twist, and K 9 (11, 13) sts along the heel flap edge, place marker, K across the instep sts, place marker, pick up, twist, and K 9 (11, 13) sts along the other heel flap edge, K6 (7, 9).

GUSSET RND 2: K to within 2 sts of marker, K2 tog, move marker, K across instep to marker, move marker, SSK, K to end.

GUSSET RND 3: K.

Rep Gusset Rnds 2–3 until 42 (48, 60) sts rem.

FOOT Work even until foot measures from the gusset edge: Youth Shoe Size 1–2: 3½ in., Youth Shoe Size 3–4: 4 in., Women's Shoe Size 5–6: 4½ in., Women's Shoe Size 7–8: 5½ in., Women's Shoe Size 9–10: 6 in., Men's Shoe Size 8–9: 6½ in., Men's Shoe Size 10–11: 7 in., Men's Shoe Size 12–13: 7½ in.

LAST FOOT RND: K11 (12, 15), place marker, K21 (24, 30), place marker, K10 (12, 15).

TOE **WEDGE TOE DECREASE RND 1:** K to within 2 sts of first marker, K2 tog, move marker, SSK, K to within 2 sts of 2nd marker, K2 tog, move marker, SSK, K to end. (4 sts dec)

WEDGE TOE DECREASE RND 2: K.

Rep Wedge Toe Decrease Rnds 1–2 until 22 (24, 28) sts rem. You may need to K to a marker or side.

Cut yarn, leaving a 12-in. tail. Close rem sts with Kitchener st.

FINISHING With matching yarn, using Mattress st, sew the back cuff seam. Weave all loose ends in on the inside of the sock. Wash and block the socks.

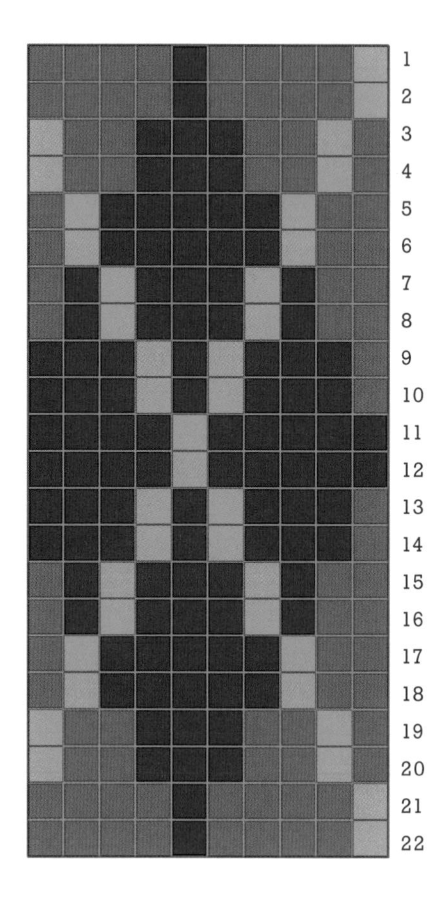

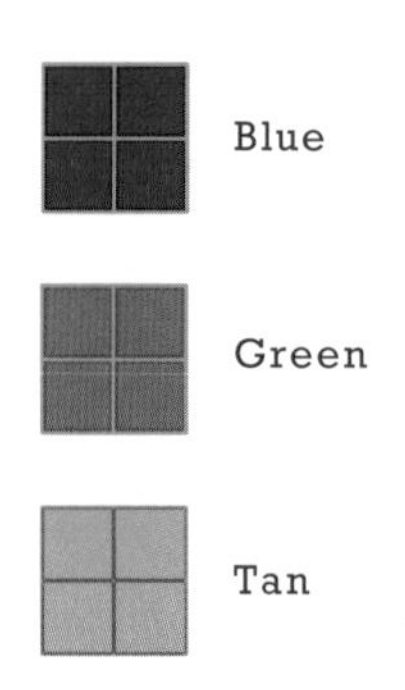

ARGYLE BORDER SOCK CHART

One-Skein CHECKERBOARD SOCK

The Noro Kureyon Sock Yarn seems to have been invented for this design, knitted with just one ball of yarn. Noro's long pattern repeats mean that you are unlikely to have the same color coming from the inside and the outside of the ball at the same time (and if you do, just snip one of the color strands and tie on again with the next color in the repeat) (shown at right knit in Noro Kureyon Sock Yarn).

PATTERN DIFFICULTY: Advanced
YARN: Superfine Weight Yarn (CYCA 1), approx. 460 yd. Self-striping
YARN WEIGHT: Superfine (CYCA 1)
NEEDLES: Size 2 (U.S.)/ 2.75 mm, or size needed to obtain gauge 1 or 2 circulars or 4 or 5 dpns, as desired
1 size 3 (U.S.)/3.25 mm needle for casting on
TOOLS: Large-eye blunt needle
PATTERN SIZES: Youth (1–2, 3–4), Women's Average, Women's Wide, (5–6, 7–8, 9–10)
MEASUREMENTS: Cuff Length: Youth: 5¼ in., Women's Average and Wide: 6¼ in.; Cuff Width: Youth: 3 in., Women's Average: 3¾ in., Women's Wide: 4¼ in.; Heel-to-Toe Length: Youth Shoe Size 1–2: 7½ in., Youth Shoe Size 3–4: 7¾ in., Women's Shoe Size 5–6: 8¼ in., Women's Shoe Size 7–8: 9¼ in., Women's Shoe Size 9–10: 10¼ in.
HEEL STYLE: Short Row
GAUGE: 10 sts = 1 in., 9 rnds = 1 in. over Checkerboard Pattern

CHECKERBOARD PATTERN (4-st, 4-rnd repeat) Wind the yarn into 2 balls or use 1 yarn strand from the outside of the ball and 1 from the center of the ball, knitting from the same ball throughout. The yarns will be designated OB (outside the ball) and IB (inside the ball). If using yarn from separate balls, designate one OB and one IB.

RNDS 1–2: *K 2 sts IB, K 2 sts OB*, rep around.

RNDS 3–4: *K 2 sts OB, K 2 sts IB*, rep around.

With a size 3 needle, and using the IB strand, CO 52 (60, 64) sts. Distribute on size 2 needles, 1 or 2 circulars or 3 or 4 dpns, as desired. Without twisting, join.

CUFF Work 12 (14, 16) rnds in K2, P2 ribbing.

NEXT RND: K, inc 8 (12, 20) sts evenly spaced in rnd. (60, 72, 84 sts)

Work Checkerboard Pattern until cuff measures 5¼ in. (6¼ in.) long, ending with either Rnd 2 or 4.

HEEL SETUP Work 15 sts in the established patt. Place the next 30 (42, 54) sts on a separate needle or holder for the instep. Place the rem 15 sts on the first needle for the heel. (30 heel sts)

HEEL Holding both the IB and OB strands together throughout, work a 30-st Short-Row Heel (see pages 174–175).

FOOT SETUP Sl 1, K14, begin new rnd at center of heel. Working again with just 1 strand of yarn at a time, begin established Checkerboard Pattern.

Work established Checkerboard Pattern until foot measures: Youth Shoe Size 1–2: 3½ in., Youth Shoe Size 3–4: 4 in., Women's Shoe Size 5–6: 4½ in., Women's Shoe Size 7–8: 5¼ in., Women's Shoe Size 9–10: 5½ in.

TOE, WOMEN'S WIDE ONLY

TOE DECREASE RND 1: *K12, K2 tog*, rep around. (78 sts rem)

TOE DECREASE RND 2 AND ALL EVEN RNDS: K.

TOE DECREASE RND 3: *K11, K2 tog*, rep around. (72 sts rem)

TOE, ALL SIZES Work toe holding both the IB and OB strands together throughout. Work a 60 (72, 72)-st Star Toe as instructed on pages 30–31.

FINISHING Weave all ends in on the inside of the sock. Wash and block the socks.

Nordic Style
Adult Sock

Nordic-Style ADULT SOCK

Traditional Nordic black-and-white patterning has been used for these strikingly beautiful socks, sized for men and women (shown at left knit in Regia 4-Ply).

PATTERN DIFFICULTY: Advanced

YARN: Superfine Weight Yarn (CYCA 1), approx. 230 (450) yd. Black and 230 (450) yd. White

YARN WEIGHT: Superfine (CYCA 1)

NEEDLES: Size 2 (U.S.)/ 2.75 mm, or size needed to obtain gauge 1 or 2 circulars or 4 or 5 dpns, as desired
1 size 3 (U.S.)/3.25 mm needle for casting on

TOOLS: Large-eye blunt needle, stitch markers

PATTERN SIZES: Women's (5–6, 7–8, 9–10), Men's (9, 10–11, 12–13)

MEASUREMENTS: Cuff Length: Women's: 6¾ in., Men's: 7½ in.; Cuff Width: Women's: 4 in., Men's: 5 in.; Heel-to-Toe Length: Women's Shoe Size 5–6: 7¼ in., Women's Shoe Size 7–8: 8¼ in., Women's Shoe Size 9–10: 9¼ in., Men's Shoe Size 9–10: 9½ in., Men's Shoe Size 11–12: 10 in., Men's Shoe Size 13: 11 in.

HEEL STYLE: Flap and Gusset

GAUGE: 9.5 sts = 1 in., 10 sts = 1 in. over Stranded Knitting

Note: Hold the unused color on the inside of the sock, stranding it loosely behind the work. Do not strand more than 6 sts without winding the unused yarn around the active yarn. Leave at least a 3-in. tail when changing colors.

With White and size 3 needle, CO 76 (96) sts. Divide on size 2 needles, 1 or 2 circulars or 3 or 4 dpns, as desired. Without twisting sts, join.

RIBBING RNDS 1–2: *K2, P2*, rep around.

RIBBING RNDS 3–16: *K2 White, P2 Black*, rep around.

NEXT RND, WOMEN'S: K with White.

NEXT RND, MEN'S: K with White, dec 1 st in rnd. (95 sts)

CUFF Follow chart, beginning where indicated for your size, until cuff measures 6¾ in. (7½ in.).

HEEL SETUP Working *K1 White, K1 Black*, work 18 (20) sts. Place next 40 (55) sts on a separate holder or needle for the instep. Place the remaining 18 (20) sts with the first sts for the heel.

HEEL FLAP ROW 1: Turn. Sl 1, P across, working in alternate Black and White sts. Turn.

HEEL FLAP ROW 2: Sl 1, K across, working in alternate Black and White sts. Turn.

Work Heel Flap until it measures 1½ in. (2 in.), end with P row.

HEEL Cut Black. Work a 36 (40)-st Flap and Gusset heel with White, as instructed on page 25.

GUSSET With White, Sl 1, K9 (11). Begin new rnd at center of Heel.

GUSSET RND 1: With White, K10 (12), pick up, twist, and K 15 (20) sts along heel flap edge, picking up the sts on the 2nd st, not the Sl st edge. Place marker. Tie on Black, work across instep sts in established charted patt; work the extra sts on either side of the charted motif in alternate Black and White. Cut Black. Place marker. With White, pick up, twist, and K 15 (20) sts along heel flap edge, K the rem 10 (12) sts.

GUSSET RND 2: Tie on Black, work alternating Black and White sts, work to within 2 sts of marker, K2 tog, move marker, work across instep in established charted patt, move marker, SSK, work to end of rnd, alternating Black and White sts.

GUSSET RND 3: Work in alternating Black and White sts to marker, move marker, work instep in established charted patt, move marker, work alternating Black and White sts to end of rnd. Rep Gusset Rnds 2–3 until 76 (95) sts rem.

FOOT Work foot as established, charted patt on instep, alternating Black and White sts on sole, until 2 full reps have been worked for Women's, and 2½ reps have been worked for Men's. Work all sts in Black and White alternating sts, until foot measures: Women's Shoe Size 5–6: 4 in., Women's Shoe Size 7–8: 5 in., Women's Shoe Size 9–10: 5½ in., Men's Shoe Size 9: 5½ in., Men's Shoe Size 10–11: 6 in., Men's Shoe Size 12–13: 6½ in.

Note: Alternating sts may not match up perfectly at the instep when you begin the alternating Black and White patt across the instep. You may have to work 2 sts in the same color for the established patt to continue on the sole.

LAST FOOT RND, MEN'S SIZE: Dec 1 st in rnd. (94 sts rem)

TOE **WEDGE TOE RND 1:** Work 19 (24) sts in established alternating Black and White patt, place marker, work in established alternating Black and White patt until 19 (23) sts rem, place marker, finish rnd.

WEDGE TOE RND 2: Work in established alternating Black and White patt to within 2 sts of marker, K2, move marker, K2, work established alternating patt to within 2 sts of next marker, K2, move marker, K2, work established alternating patt to end.

WEDGE TOE RND 3: Work established alternating patt to within 2 sts of marker, K2 tog, move marker, SSK, work established alternating patt to within 2 sts of next marker, K2 tog, move marker, SSK, work established alternating patt to end.

Rep Wedge Toe Rnds 2–3 until 32 (38) sts rem. Work in patt to next marker.

FINISHING Divide sts on 2 needles and close the toe with Kitchener st. Weave all loose ends in on the inside of the sock. Wash and block the socks.

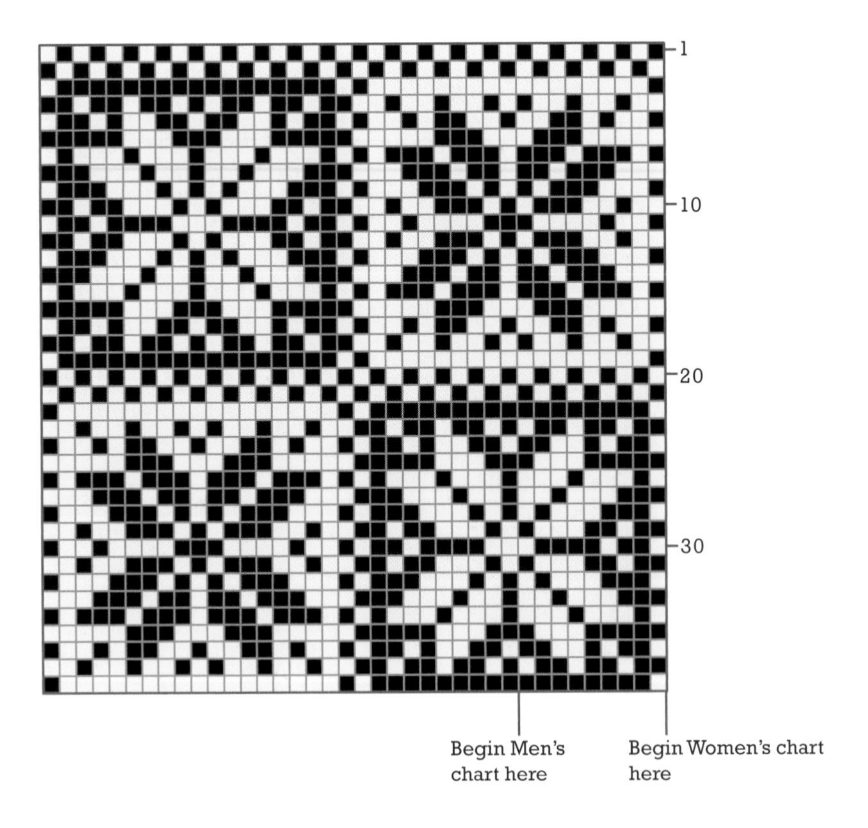

NORDIC-STYLE ADULT SOCK CHART

Snowflake HOUSE SOCK

The picot hem and stranded toe and heel make this colorful sock design a step outside the ordinary. One adult size fits most foot widths, and one child size fits most child/youth foot widths (shown on page 17 knit in Knit Picks Telemark).

PATTERN DIFFICULTY: Advanced
YARN: Fine Weight Yarn (CYCA 2), approx. 100 (200) yd. Green, 100 yd. each of Cream, Orange, Tan, and Blue
YARN WEIGHT: Fine (CYCA 2)
NEEDLES: Size 4 (U.S.)/3.5 mm, or size needed to obtain gauge 1 or 2 circulars or 4 or 5 dpns, as desired
TOOLS: Large-eye blunt needle, stitch markers
PATTERN SIZES: Child/Youth (10–11, 12–13, 1–2, 3–4), Adult (Women's 5–6, 7–8, 9–10, Men's 9, 10–11, 12–13)
MEASUREMENTS: Cuff Length from Picot Rnd: Child: 5¾ in., Adult: 6½ in.; Cuff Width: Child: 3 in., Adult: 4¼ in.; Heel-to-Toe Length: Child Shoe Size 10–11: 5¾ in., Child Shoe Size 12–13: 6¼ in., Youth Shoe Size 1–2: 6½ in., Youth Shoe Size 3–4: 6¾ in., Women's Shoe Size 5–6: 9 in., Women's Shoe Size 7–8: 9½ in., Women's Shoe Size 9–10: 10 in., Men's Shoe Size 9: 10½ in., Size 10–11: 11 in., Men's Shoe Size 12–13: 12 in.
HEEL STYLE: Flap and Gusset, Stranded Flap
GAUGE: 6.5 sts = 1 in., 7.5 rnds = 1 in. over Stranded Knitting

Note: Tie new colors on at the beginning of the round; leave at least a 3-in. tail at each tie. Strand unused colors loosely on the back of the work. Do not strand unused yarn more than 5 stitches without twisting the yarn strands on the back of the work.

With Tangelo and size 4 needles, CO 36 (48) sts. Divide on 1 or 2 circulars or 3 or 4 dpns, as desired. Without twisting sts, join.

RNDS 1–5: K.

RND 6, PICOT RND: *YO, K2 tog*, rep around.

RND 7: K, working each YO as a stitch.

RNDS 8–11: K.

CUFF Begin Cuff Chart from the top.

CUFF CHART RND 1: Inc 6 (8) sts evenly spaced in rnd. (42, 56 sts)

Work cuff, following Cuff chart, repeating the lower Cuff chart bands as needed, until cuff measures 5¾ in. (6½ in.) from Picot Rnd.

ADULT SIZE ONLY: End cuff on 2nd to last rnd of the last Green/Orange border.

HEEL SETUP K 10 (14) sts. Child Size Only: Tie on Green.

Place the next 22 (28) sts on a separate holder or needle for the instep. Place the rem 10 (14) sts with the heel sts.

HEEL FLAP: Work the heel flap as shown in the proper size chart.

HEEL FLAP WS ROWS: Sl 1, P across according to the chart, turn.

HEEL FLAP RS ROWS: Sl 1, K across according to the chart, turn.

End with a WS row.

HEEL Work a 20 (24)-st Flap and Gusset Heel with Green, as instructed on pages 26–27.

GUSSET **GUSSET RND 1:** K6 (8), pick up, twist, and K 10 (12) sts along heel flap edge, place marker, K across instep sts following chart in established manner, place marker, pick up, twist, and K 10 (12) sts along other heel flap edge, K 6 (8) sts.

GUSSET RND 2: Work charted border, K to within

2 sts of marker, SSK, move marker, K across instep sts following chart in established manner, move marker, K2 tog, K to end. (2 sts dec)

GUSSET RND 3: K.

Rep Gusset Rnds 2–3 until 44 (56) sts rem. (**Note:** The Child Size will have 2 more sts on the foot than on the cuff.)

Work foot, following the charted borders, until foot measures from the beginning of the gusset: Child Shoe Size 10–11: 3 in., Child Shoe Size 12–13: 2½ in., Youth Shoe Size 1–2: 4 in., Youth Shoe Size 3–4: 4 in., Women's Shoe Size 5–6: 4 in., Women's Shoe Size 7–8: 5 in., Women's Shoe Size 9–10: 5½ in., Men's Shoe Size 9: 6 in., Men's Shoe Size 10–11: 6½ in., Men's Shoe Size 12–13: 7 in.

TOE Work Toe chart for your sock size, making sure that the toe lines up properly with the heel. SSK the decs on the right sides of the charts, and K2tog decs on the left sides of the charts. Close the opening with Kitchener st.

FINISHING Weave in all loose ends on the inside of the sock. Fold the Picot Hem in and stitch down with matching yarn. Wash and block the socks.

SNOWFLAKE HOUSE SOCK CHARTS

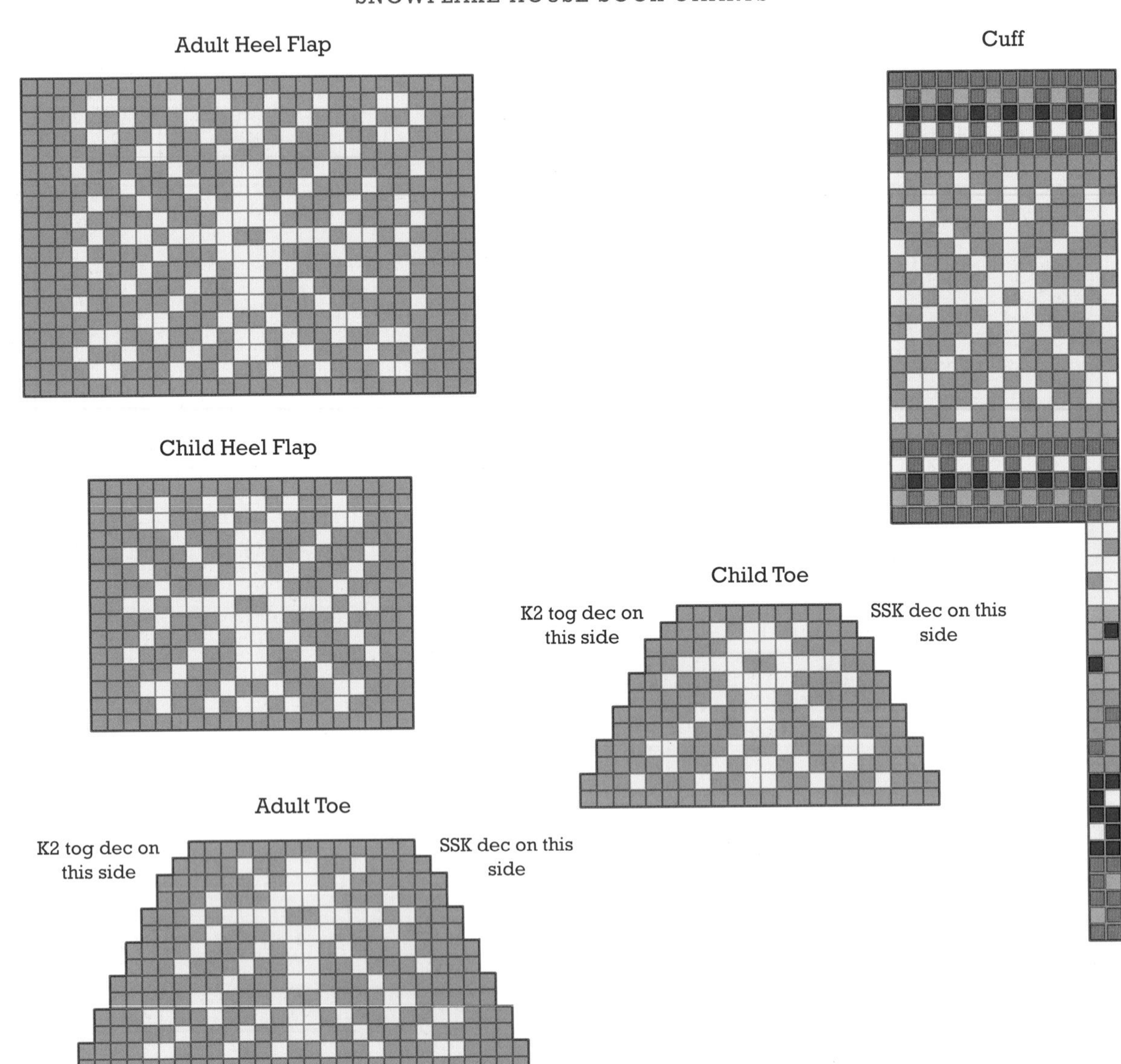

Holiday Garland SOCK

Worked in red and green with embroidered golden highlights, these socks are perfect for the holidays—warm and cushy, with a lovely halo from the mohair content in the recommended yarn. Change up the colorway, and they're great for any fall or winter day (shown at left knit in ShibuiKnits Merino Kid).

PATTERN DIFFICULTY: Intermediate

YARN: Medium Weight Yarn (CYCA 4), approx. 200 (200, 200, 200, 400) yd. Green; 200 (200, 200, 200, 400) yd. Red; 5 yd. Yellow

YARN WEIGHT: Medium (CYCA 4)

NEEDLES: Size 5 (U.S.)/3.75 mm, or size needed to obtain gauge 1 or 2 circulars or 4 or 5 dpns, as desired

TOOLS: Large-eye blunt needle

PATTERN SIZES: Child (10–11, 12–13), Youth (1–2, 3–4), Women's Average, Women's Wide (5–6, 7–8, 9–10), Men's Average (8–9, 10–11, 12–13)

MEASUREMENTS: Cuff Length: Child: 4½ in., Youth: 5½ in., Women's: 6½ in., Men's: 7½ in.; Cuff Width: Child: 2¾ in., Youth: 3¼ in., Women's Average: 3¾ in., Women's Wide: 4¼ in., Men's: 4¾ in.; Heel-to-Toe Length: Child Shoe Size 10–11: 5½ in., Child Shoe Size 12–13: 6¼ in., Youth Shoe Size 1–2: 7 in., Youth Shoe Size 3–4: 7½ in., Women's Shoe Size 5–6: 9 in., Women's Shoe Size 7–8: 9½ in., Women's Shoe Size 9–10: 10 in., Men's Shoe Size 8–9: 10½ in., Men's Shoe Size 10–11: 11 in., Men's Shoe Size 12–13: 12 in.

HEEL STYLE: Short Row

GAUGE: 7 sts = 1 in., 7 rnds = 1 in. over Stranded Knitting

Note: Hold the unused color on the inside of the sock, stranding it loosely behind the work. Do not strand more than 5 sts without winding the unused yarn around the active yarn. Leave at least a 3-in. tail when changing colors.

Note: If you prefer not to Duplicate stitch the yellow highlights, you may knit with three strands for those rows. Be sure to strand the unused yarns loosely behind the work.

Note: Work **Women's Narrow** as for **Youth**; adjust foot and cuff length for shoe size.

With Red and size 5 needles, CO 40 (48, 52, 60, 66) sts. Distribute on 1 or 2 circulars or 3 or 4 dpns, as desired. Without twisting the sts, join.

RIBBING RND 1: *K2, P2* around.

RIBBING RNDS 2–3: Tie on Green. *K2 Red, P2 Green*, rep around.

RIBBING RNDS 4–5: *K2 Green, P2 Red*, rep around.

Continue in established patt, alternating colors, until ribbing is 7 (9, 11, 11, 13) rnds long.

NEXT RND, ALL SIZES: Rep Ribbing Rnd 1 with Red.

NEXT RND, CHILD AND WOMEN'S AVERAGE SIZES ONLY: K with Red, inc 2 sts evenly spaced in rnd. (42, 54 sts)

NEXT RND, ALL OTHER SIZES: K with Red.

Follow chart, beginning at Rnd 2 for first repeat, and then from Rnd 1 thereafter. You may work the Yellow highlights by knitting with 3 strands, or you may work those squares with the background color and embroider the highlights with a Duplicate st after finishing the sock.

Work the cuff until it measures 4½ in. (5½ in., 6½ in., 6½ in., 7½ in.).

HEEL SETUP Work 10 (12, 13, 15, 16) sts in established charted patt. Place the next 22 (24, 28, 30, 34) sts on a separate needle or holder for the instep, place the rem 10 (12, 13, 15, 16) sts with the first for the heel. Cut Red, and knit the heel with Green.

HEEL Work a 20 (24, 26, 30, 32)-st Short-Row Heel as instructed on pages 28–30.

FOOT SETUP Sl 1, K 9 (11, 12, 14, 15) sts. Tie on Red, and begin new rnd at the center of the heel.

FOOT Work the foot, continuing in the established charted patt, until the foot measures: Child Shoe Size 10–11: 3 in., Child Shoe Size 12–13: 3¾ in., Youth Shoe Size 1–2: 4¼ in., Youth Shoe Size 3–4: 4¾ in., Women's Shoe Size 5–6: 5¼ in., Women's Shoe Size 7–8: 5¾ in., Women's Shoe Size 9–10: 6¼ in., Men's Shoe Size 8–9: 6¼ in., Men's Shoe Size 10–12: 6¾ in., Men's Shoe Size 13: 7 in.

TOE Cut Red. Work a 42 (48, 54, 60, 66)-st Star Toe with Green, as instructed on page 31.

FINISHING If needed, thread Yellow yarn in a large eye needle and Duplicate st the highlights as charted. Weave all loose ends in on the inside of the sock. Wash and block the socks.

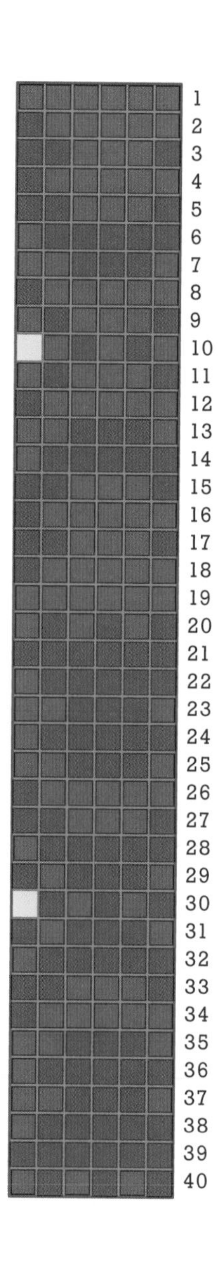

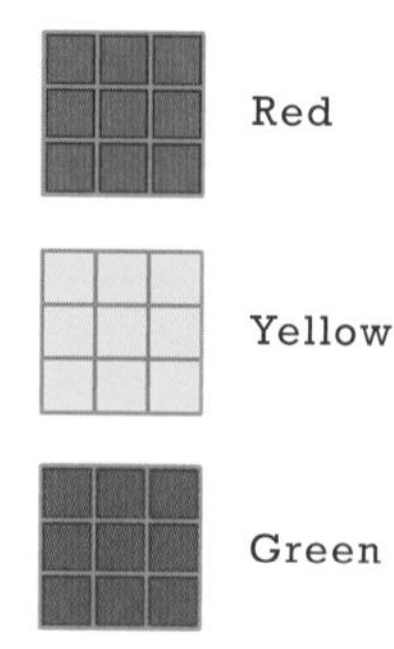

HOLIDAY GARLAND SOCK CHART

Mosaic Tile SOCK

This design reminds me of mosaic tiles. I love the allover repeating pattern and the intricate two-color design. This chart has a short repeat and is much easier to knit than it looks, with very few ends to weave in when you're finished (shown on page 23 knit in ShibuiKnits Sock).

PATTERN DIFFICULTY: Advanced

YARN: Superfine Weight Yarn (CYCA 1), approx. 190 (190, 380, 380) yd. Pink; 190 (190, 190, 380) yd. Blue

YARN WEIGHT: Superfine (CYCA 1)

NEEDLES: Size 2 (U.S.)/2.75 mm, or size needed to obtain gauge 1 or 2 circulars or 4 or 5 dpns, as desired

TOOLS: Large-eye blunt needle, stitch markers

PATTERN SIZES: Child (10–11, 12–13), Youth (1–2, 3–4), Women's Average, Women's Wide, (5–6, 7–8, 9–10)

MEASUREMENTS: Cuff Length: Child: 4¼ in., Youth: 5¼ in., Women's Average and Wide: 6¼ in.; Cuff Width: Child: 2½ in., Youth: 3 in., Women's Average: 3¾ in., Women's Wide: 4¼ in.; Heel-to-Toe Foot Length: Child Shoe Size 10–11: 5¾ in., Child Shoe Size 12–13: 6¼ in., Youth Shoe Size 1–2: 7½ in., Youth Shoe Size 3–4: 7¾ in., Women's Shoe Size 5–6: 8¼ in., Women's Shoe Size 7–8: 9¼ in., Women's Shoe Size 9–10: 10¼ in.

HEEL STYLE: Flap and Gusset

GAUGE: 10 sts = 1 in., 9 rnds = 1 in. over Stranded Knitting

Note: Hold the unused color on the inside of the sock, stranding it loosely behind the work. Do not strand more than 6 sts without winding the unused yarn around the active yarn. Leave at least a 3-in. tail when changing colors.

With Pink and size 2 needles, CO 48 (60, 72, 84) sts. Without twisting the sts, join. Work 10 rnds in Stockinette st.

PICOT RND 1: Tie on Blue. K around.

PICOT RND 2: With Blue, *YO, K2 tog*, rep around.

PICOT RND 3: With Blue, K around, knitting each YO as a st.

PICOT RND 4: With Pink, K.

Work chart, beginning at Rnd 1, continue through Rnd 34. Rep Rnds 21–34 until otherwise noted. Continue until cuff measures from Picot Rnd 2: Child: 4¼ in., Youth: 5¼ in., Women's Average and Wide: 6¼ in.

HEEL SETUP Work the first 12 (15, 18, 20) sts in the established patt. Place the next 24 (30, 36, 44) sts on a separate needle or holder for the instep.

Place the rem 12 (15, 18, 20) sts on the first needle for the heel (24, 30, 36, 40 heel sts).

HEEL FLAP ROW 1: Turn. Sl 1, P across, alternating Pink and Blue. Turn.

HEEL FLAP ROW 2: Sl 1, K across, alternating Pink and Blue in vertical rows. Turn.

Rep Heel Flap Rows 1–2, 10 (12, 14, 16) times more. End with a P row.

HEEL With Pink, work a 24 (30, 36, 40)-st Flap and Gusset Heel as shown on pages 25–26.

GUSSET Sl 1, K 6 (8, 9, 11) sts. Begin new rnd at center of heel.

GUSSET RND 1: With Pink, K 7 (9, 10, 12) sts, pick up, twist, and K 10 (12, 14, 16) sts along the heel flap edge (picking up the sts from the first K st, not the Sl st edge), place marker, tie on Blue, and work across the instep sts in the established patt following the chart, place marker. Cut Blue. With Pink, pick up, twist, and K 10 (12, 14, 16) sts along the other heel flap edge (picking up the sts from the first K st, not the Sl st edge), K7 (9, 10, 12).

GUSSET RND 2: Tie on Blue. K, alternating Pink and Blue, to within 2 sts of the marker. With Pink, K2 tog, move marker, work across instep sts in established patt, following the chart, move marker, SSK with Pink, work rem sts alternating Pink and Blue.
(2 sts dec)

GUSSET RND 3: K, working the gusset and sole sts in established alternating Pink and Blue patt, work instep in established patt following the chart.

Rep Gusset Rnds 2–3 until 48 (60, 72, 84) sts rem. Redistribute sts on needles if desired.

FOOT Work foot in established patt (alternating Pink and Blue on the sole, following the chart on the instep) until foot measures: Child Shoe Size 10–11: 2 in., Child Shoe Size 12–13: 2½ in., Youth Shoe Size 1–2: 3 in., Youth Shoe Size 3–4: 3½ in., Women's Shoe Size 5–6: 4 in., Women's Shoe Size 7–8: 5 in., Women's Shoe Size 9–10: 5½ in.

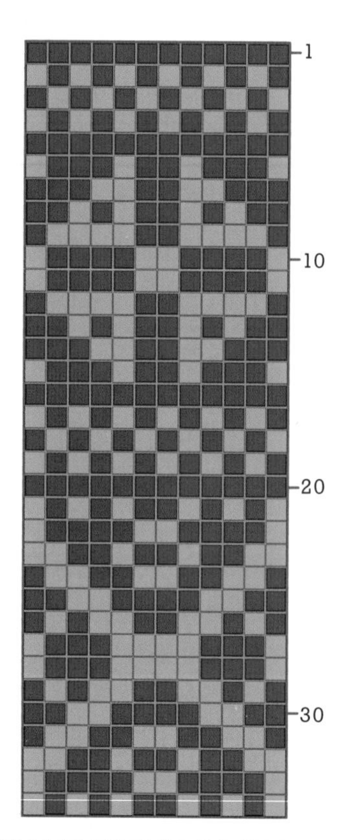

MOSAIC TILE SOCK CHART

ALL SIZES: Work Charted Rnds 1–5.

On last Charted Rnd, K 12 (15, 18, 21) sts in established patt, place marker, K 24 (30, 36, 42) sts in established patt, place marker, K rem 12 (15, 18, 21) sts.

TOE **TOE DECREASE RND 1:** K, alternating Pink and Blue, to within 2 sts of the first marker, K2 tog with Pink, move marker, SSK with Pink, K, alternating Pink and Blue, to within 2 sts of the 2nd marker, K2 tog with Pink, move marker, SSK with Pink, K to end, alternating Pink and Blue. (4 sts dec)

TOE DECREASE RND 2: K, alternating Pink and Blue as established, working the sts on either side of both markers with Pink.

Rep Toe Decrease Rnds 1–2 until 24 (32, 36, 40) sts rem, using Pink only on the last rnd. If the sts are not already divided in half, divide them on 2 needles, so that the decs are at either side of each needle. You may need to K to one marker. Close the toe with Kitchener st.

FINISHING Fold hem in at the picot edge, and stitch down on the inside of the sock. Weave all the loose ends in on the inside of the sock. Wash and block the socks.

AFTERTHOUGHT HEELS

An Afterthought Heel is knitted after the body of the sock has been finished. If you're knitting in the round, you indicate the heel location with a length of waste yarn knit into the sock as you construct it. Remove that waste yarn and pick up the live stitch loops to knit them in the round, the same way you do for a Wedge Toe. Individual instructions for Afterthought Heels are included as necessary in the patterns, though you can also refer to the Wedge Toe section of this chapter for further instructions.

You can also knit Afterthought Heel socks flat, with two needles. Indicate the heel location by binding off the heel stitches on one row, then casting on the same number of stitches on the next row, leaving a precise opening for you to pick up the heel stitches after the rest of the sock is completed.

After binding off a Two-Needle Afterthought Heel, you close the back seam with a Kitchener st, and then sew the remaining sock seam with a Mattress st. Individual instructions for Two-Needle Afterthought Heels are included as necessary in the patterns, though you can also refer to the Wedge Toe section of this chapter for instructions.

FLAP & GUSSET HEELS

THE HEEL SETUP The patterns here use two methods for getting ready to knit Flap and Gusset Heels. One method selects the heel flap stitches from the first stitches on the needle, which changes the location of the beginning of the round after the heel is completed. The other centers the heel stitches on the back of the cuff. Each pattern specifies which cuff stitches will become the heel stitches. Follow your chosen pattern instructions for the heel setup.

THE HEEL FLAP In general, you work a heel flap over roughly half of the total stitches. For most patterns, you work it back and forth by setting the instep stitches on a separate needle or holder, and working with just the heel stitches. You slip the first stitch of every row, and purl the rest on the wrong

side. You work a combination of *slip one stitch, knit one stitch* (Sl 1, K1) on the right side.

Flap and Gusset Heel Instructions

Though you work this type of heel with short rows, it is different from what is generally termed a *Short-Row Heel.* There are many styles of Flap and Gusset Heels, but this style appears throughout the patterns in this booklet.

40-Stitch Flap and Gusset Heel

After completing the Heel Flap, and ending with a wrong side (purl) row, turn:

HEEL TURN ROW 1: Sl 1, K24, K2 tog, K1, turn. (Leave rem sts on the needle.)

HEEL TURN ROW 2: Sl 1, P11, P2 tog, P1, turn.

HEEL TURN ROW 3: Sl 1, K12, K2 tog, K1, turn.

HEEL TURN ROW 4: Sl 1, P13, P2 tog, P1, turn.

HEEL TURN ROW 5: Sl 1, K14, K2 tog, K1, turn.

HEEL TURN ROW 6: Sl 1, P15, P2 tog, P1, turn.

HEEL TURN ROW 7: Sl 1, K16, K2 tog, K1, turn.

HEEL TURN ROW 8: Sl 1, P17, P2 tog, P1, turn.

HEEL TURN ROW 9: Sl 1, K18, K2 tog, K1, turn.

HEEL TURN ROW 10: Sl 1, P19, P2 tog, P1, turn.

HEEL TURN ROW 11: Sl 1, K20, K2 tog, K1, turn.

HEEL TURN ROW 12: Sl 1, P21, P2 tog, P1, turn.

HEEL TURN ROW 13: Sl 1, K22, K2 tog, K1, turn.

HEEL TURN ROW 14: Sl 1, P23, P2 tog, P1, turn.

HEEL TURN ROW 15: Sl 1, K23, K2 tog, turn.

HEEL TURN ROW 16: Sl 1, P22, P2 tog, turn. (24 sts rem)

GUSSET SETUP: Sl 1, K11. Begin new rnd at the center of the heel. Change colors if instructed in individual pattern. Redistribute sts on needles as desired.

36-Stitch Flap and Gusset Heel

After completing the Heel Flap, and ending with a wrong side (purl) row, turn:

HEEL TURN ROW 1: Sl 1, K21, K2 tog, K1, turn. (Leave rem sts on the needle.)

HEEL TURN ROW 2: Sl 1, P9, P2 tog, P1, turn.

Work as for 40-Stitch Flap and Gusset Heel until 22 sts rem.

GUSSET SETUP: Sl 1, K10. Begin new rnd at the center of the heel. Change colors if indicated in individual pattern. Redistribute sts on needles as desired.

34-Stitch Flap and Gusset Heel

After completing the Heel Flap, and ending with a wrong side (purl) row, turn:

HEEL TURN ROW 1: Sl 1, K21, K2 tog, K1, turn. (Leave rem sts on the needle.)

HEEL TURN ROW 2: Sl 1, P11, P2 tog, P1, turn.

Work as for 40-Stitch Flap and Gusset Heel until 22 sts rem.

GUSSET SETUP: Sl 1, K10. Begin new rnd at the center of the heel. Change colors if instructed to in individual pattern. Redistribute sts on needles as desired.

32-Stitch Flap and Gusset Heel

After completing the Heel Flap, and ending with a wrong side (purl) row, turn:

HEEL TURN ROW 1: Sl 1, K19, K2 tog, K1, turn. (Leave rem sts on the needle.)

HEEL TURN ROW 2: Sl 1, P9, P2 tog, P1, turn.

Work as for 40-Stitch Flap and Gusset Heel until 20 sts rem.

GUSSET SETUP: Sl 1, K9. Begin new rnd at the center of the heel. Change colors if instructed in individual pattern. Redistribute sts on needles as desired.

30-Stitch Flap and Gusset Heel

After completing the Heel Flap, and ending with a wrong side (purl) row, turn:

HEEL TURN ROW 1: Sl 1, K18, K2 tog, K1, turn. (Leave rem sts on the needle.)

HEEL TURN ROW 2: Sl 1, P9, P2 tog, P1, turn.

Work as for 40-Stitch Flap and Gusset Heel until 18 sts rem.

GUSSET SETUP: Sl 1, K8. Begin new rnd at the center of the heel. Change colors if instructed in individual pattern. Redistribute sts on needles as desired.

28-Stitch Flap and Gusset Heel

After completing the Heel Flap, and ending with a wrong side (purl) row, turn:

HEEL TURN ROW 1: Sl 1, K16, K2 tog, K1, turn. (Leave rem sts on the needle.)

HEEL TURN ROW 2: Sl 1, P7, P2 tog, P1, turn.

Work as for 40-Stitch Flap and Gusset Heel until 16 sts rem.

GUSSET SETUP: Sl 1, K7. Begin the new rnd at the center of the heel. Change colors if indicated in individual pattern. Redistribute sts on needles as desired.

26-Stitch Flap and Gusset Heel

After completing the Heel Flap, and ending with a wrong side (purl) row, turn:

HEEL TURN ROW 1: Sl 1, K14, K2 tog, K1, turn. (Leave rem sts on the needle.)

HEEL TURN ROW 2: Sl 1, P5, P2 tog, P1, turn.

Work as for 40-Stitch Flap and Gusset Heel until 14 sts rem.

GUSSET SETUP: Sl 1, K6. Begin the new rnd at the center of the heel. Change colors if indicated in individual pattern. Redistribute sts on needles as desired.

24-Stitch Flap and Gusset Heel

After completing the Heel Flap, and ending with a wrong side (purl) row, turn:

HEEL TURN ROW 1: Sl 1, K13, K2 tog, K1, turn. (Leave rem sts on the needle.)

HEEL TURN ROW 2: Sl 1, P5, P2 tog, P1, turn.

Work as for 40-Stitch Flap and Gusset Heel until 14 sts rem.

GUSSET SETUP: Sl 1, K6. Begin the new rnd at the center of the heel. Change colors if instructed in individual pattern. Redistribute sts on needles as desired.

22-Stitch Flap and Gusset Heel

After completing the Heel Flap, and ending with a wrong side (purl) row, turn:

HEEL TURN ROW 1: Sl 1, K12, K2 tog, K1, turn. (Leave rem sts on the needle.)

HEEL TURN ROW 2: Sl 1, P5, P2 tog, P1, turn.

Work as for 40-Stitch Flap and Gusset Heel until 12 sts rem.
GUSSET SETUP: Sl 1, K5. New rnd begins at center of heel. Change colors if indicated in individual pattern. Redistribute sts on needles as desired.

20-Stitch Flap and Gusset Heel

After completing the Heel Flap, and ending with a wrong side (purl) row, turn:
HEEL TURN ROW 1: Sl 1, K11, K2 tog, K1, turn. (Leave rem sts on the needle.)
HEEL TURN ROW 2: Sl 1, P5, P2 tog, P1, turn.
Work as for 40-Stitch Flap and Gusset Heel until 12 sts rem.
GUSSET SETUP: Sl 1, K5. New rnd begins at center of heel. Change colors if instructed in the individual pattern. Redistribute sts on needles as desired.

18-Stitch Flap and Gusset Heel

After completing the Heel Flap, and ending with a wrong side (purl) row, turn:
HEEL TURN ROW 1: Sl 1, K10, K2 tog, K1, turn. (Leave rem sts on the needle.)
HEEL TURN ROW 2: Sl 1, P5, P2 tog, P1, turn.
Work as for 40-Stitch Flap and Gusset Heel until 10 sts rem.
GUSSET SETUP: Sl 1, K4. New rnd begins at center of heel. Change colors if instructed in the individual pattern. Redistribute sts on needles as desired.

16-Stitch Flap and Gusset Heel

After completing the Heel Flap, and ending with a wrong side (purl) row, turn:
HEEL TURN ROW 1: Sl 1, K9, K2 tog, K1, turn. (Leave rem sts on the needle.)
HEEL TURN ROW 2: Sl 1, P5, P2 tog, P1, turn.
Work as for 40-Stitch Flap and Gusset Heel until 10 sts rem.
GUSSET SETUP: Sl 1, K4. New rnd begins at center of heel. Change colors if instructed in the individual pattern. Redistribute sts on needles as desired.

SHORT-ROW HEELS

THE HEEL SETUP The patterns in this book use two methods for getting ready to knit Short-Row Heels: after finishing the cuff (for cuff-down socks) or after finishing the foot (for toe-up socks). One method selects the heel stitches from the first stitches on the needle, which will change the location of the beginning of the round after the heel is completed. The other centers the heel stitches on the back of the cuff (or the sole, for toe-up socks). A few patterns use a different set of stitch parameters for placing the heel within established pattern repeats. Each pattern specifies which cuff (or foot) stitches will become the heel stitches. Follow your chosen pattern instructions for the heel setup.

There is no difference among worsted weight, fingering, or sport weight yarns for Short-Row Heel instructions. You can make any heel narrower (or wider) by working two more (or two less) short rows before turning.

About Short-Row Heels

The style used in this book is a No-Wrap Short-Row Heel, which I find to be very easy to knit and neat when finished, with no holes along the heel shaping.

36-Stitch Short-Row Heel

ROW 1: Turn, Sl 1, P34, turn.
ROW 2: Sl 1, K33, turn.
ROW 3: Sl 1, P32, turn.
ROW 4: Sl 1, K31, turn.
ROW 5: Sl 1, P30, turn.
ROW 6: Sl 1, K29, turn.
ROW 7: Sl 1, P28, turn.
ROW 8: Sl 1, K27, turn.

ROW 9: Sl 1, P26, turn.
ROW 10: Sl 1, K25, turn.
ROW 11: Sl 1, P24, turn.
ROW 12: Sl 1, K23, turn.
ROW 13: Sl 1, P22, turn.
ROW 14: Sl 1, K21, turn.
ROW 15: Sl 1, P20, turn.
ROW 16: Sl 1, K19, turn.
ROW 17: Sl 1, P18, turn.
ROW 18: Sl 1, K17, turn.
ROW 19: Sl 1, P16, turn.
ROW 20: Sl 1, K15, turn.
ROW 21: Sl 1, P14, turn.
ROW 22: Sl 1, K13, turn.
ROW 23: Sl 1, P12, turn.
ROW 24: Sl 1, K11, turn.
HEEL TURN ROW 1: Sl 1, P10, Sl 1, pick up loop in the gap before the next st, P the Sl st and the loop together (HTR 1), turn.
HEEL TURN ROW 2: Sl 1, K10, Sl 1, pick up and K 1 st in the gap before the next st, PSSO (HTR 2), turn.
HEEL TURN ROW 3: Sl 1, P11, work as HTR 1, turn.
HEEL TURN ROW 4: Sl 1, K12, work as HTR 2, turn.
HEEL TURN ROW 5: Sl 1, P13, work as HTR 1, turn.
HEEL TURN ROW 6: Sl 1, K14, work as HTR 2, turn.
HEEL TURN ROW 7: Sl 1, P15, work as HTR 1, turn.
HEEL TURN ROW 8: Sl 1, K16, work as HTR 2, turn.
HEEL TURN ROW 9: Sl 1, P17, work as HTR 1, turn.
HEEL TURN ROW 10: Sl 1, K18, work as HTR 2, turn.
HEEL TURN ROW 11: Sl 1, P19, work as HTR 1, turn.
HEEL TURN ROW 12: Sl 1, K20, work as HTR 2, turn.
HEEL TURN ROW 13: Sl 1, P21, work as HTR 1, turn.
HEEL TURN ROW 14: Sl 1, K22, work as HTR 2, turn.
HEEL TURN ROW 15: Sl 1, P23, work as HTR 1, turn.
HEEL TURN ROW 16: Sl 1, K24, work as HTR 2, turn.
HEEL TURN ROW 17: Sl 1, P25, work as HTR 1, turn.
HEEL TURN ROW 18: Sl 1, K26, work as HTR 2, turn.
HEEL TURN ROW 19: Sl 1, P27, work as HTR 1, turn.
HEEL TURN ROW 20: Sl 1, K28, work as HTR 2, turn.
HEEL TURN ROW 21: Sl 1, P29, work as HTR 1, turn.
HEEL TURN ROW 22: Sl 1, K30, work as HTR 2, turn.
HEEL TURN ROW 23: Sl 1, P31, work as HTR 1, turn.
HEEL TURN ROW 24: Sl 1, K32, work as HTR 2, turn.
HEEL TURN ROW 25: Sl 1, P33, Sl 1, pick up loop in gap between the instep and heel sts, work as HTR 1, turn.
HEEL TURN ROW 26: Sl 1, K17. New rnd begins in center of heel. Change yarn colors if instructed in individual pattern. K17, Sl 1, picking up the loop in the gap between the instep sts and the heel, work HTR 2. Redistribute sts on needles as desired.

32-Stitch Short-Row Heel

ROW 1: Sl 1, P30, turn.
ROW 2: Sl 1, K29, turn.
Work as for 36-St Short-Row Heel until 11 K sts rem after the slipped st.
HEEL TURN ROW 1: Sl 1, P10, Sl 1, pick up loop in the gap before the next st, P the Sl st and the loop together (HTR 1), turn.
HEEL TURN ROW 2: Sl 1, K10, Sl 1, pick up and K 1 st in the gap before the next st, PSSO (HTR 2), turn.
Work as for 36-Stitch Short-Row Heel Turn until 28 K sts rem before HTR 2.
HEEL TURN ROW 21: Sl 1, P29, picking up the loop in gap between the instep and heel sts, work as HTR 1, turn.
HEEL TURN ROW 22: Sl 1, K15, begin new rnd in center of heel unless otherwise noted in individual pattern. Change colors if indicated in pattern. With a new needle, K15, Sl 1, picking up the loop in the gap between the instep and heel sts, work as HTR 2. Redistribute stitches on needles as desired.

30-Stitch Short-Row Heel

ROW 1: Sl 1, P28, turn.
ROW 2: Sl 1, K27, turn.
Work as for 36-Stitch Short-Row Heel until 9 K sts rem after the slipped st.
HEEL TURN ROW 1: Sl 1, P8, Sl 1, pick up loop in the gap before the next st, P the Sl st and the

loop together (HTR 1), turn.
HEEL TURN ROW 2: Sl 1, K8,
Sl 1, pick up and K 1 st in the gap before the next st, PSSO (HTR 2), turn.
Work as for 36-Stitch Short-Row Heel Turn until 26 K sts rem before HTR 2.
HEEL TURN ROW 21: Sl 1, P27, picking up the loop in gap between the instep and heel sts, work as HTR 1, turn.
HEEL TURN ROW 22: Sl 1, K14, begin new rnd in center of heel unless otherwise noted in individual pattern. Change colors if indicated in pattern. K14, Sl 1, picking up the loop in the gap between the instep sts and heel sts, work as HTR 2. Redistribute sts on needles as desired.

28-Stitch Short-Row Heel

ROW 1: Sl 1, P26, turn.
ROW 2: SL 1, K25, turn.
Work as for 36-Stitch Short-Row Heel until 9 K sts rem after the slipped st.
HEEL TURN ROW 1: Sl 1, P8, Sl 1, pick up loop in the gap before the next st, P the Sl st and the loop together (HTR 1), turn.
HEEL TURN ROW 2: Sl 1, K8,
Sl 1, pick up and K 1 st in the gap before the next st, PSSO (HTR 2), turn.
Work as for 36-Stitch Short-Row Heel Turn until 24 K sts rem before HTR 2.
HEEL TURN ROW 19: Sl 1, P25, work as HTR 1, picking up the loop in the gap between the instep sts and the heel, turn.
HEEL TURN ROW 20: Sl 1, K13. New rnd begins in center of heel. Change yarn colors if instructed in individual pattern. K13, Sl 1, picking up the loop in the gap between the instep sts and the heel sts, work as HTR 2. Redistribute sts on needles as desired.

26-Stitch Short-Row Heel

ROW 1: Sl 1, P24, turn.
ROW 2: Sl 1, K23, turn.
Work as for 36-Stitch Short-Row Heel until 9 K sts rem after the slipped st.
HEEL TURN ROW 1: Sl 1, P8, Sl 1, pick up loop in the gap before the next st, P the Sl st and the loop together (HTR 1), turn.
HEEL TURN ROW 2: Sl 1, K8,
Sl 1, pick up and K 1 st in the gap before the next st, PSSO (HTR 2), turn.
Work as for 26-Stitch Short-Row Heel Turn until 22 K sts rem before HTR 2.
HEEL TURN ROW 17: Sl 1, P23,
Sl 1, picking up the loop in the gap between the instep sts and the heel sts, work as HTR 1, turn.
HEEL TURN ROW 18: Sl 1, K12. New rnd begins in center of heel. Change yarn colors if instructed in individual pattern. K12, Sl 1, picking up the loop in the gap between the instep sts and heel sts, work as HTR 2. Redistribute sts on needles as desired.

24-Stitch Short-Row Heel

ROW 1: Sl 1, P22, turn.
ROW 2: Sl 1, K21, turn.
Work as for 26-Stitch Short-Row Heel until 9 K sts rem after the slipped st.
HEEL TURN ROW 1: Sl 1, P8, work as for HTR 1, turn.
HEEL TURN ROW 2: Sl 1, K8, work as for HTR 2, turn.
Work as for 36-Stitch Short-Row Heel Turn until 20 K sts rem before HTR 2.
HEEL TURN ROW 15: Sl 1, P21, work as HTR 1, picking up the loop in the gap between the heel and the instep sts, turn.
HEEL TURN ROW 16: Sl 1, K11. New rnd begins in center of heel. Change yarn colors if instructed in individual pattern. With new needle, K11, Sl 1, picking up the loop in the gap between the instep sts and heel as, work HTR 2. Redistribute sts on needles as desired.

20-Stitch Short-Row Heel

ROW 1: Sl 1, P18, turn.
ROW 2: Sl 1, K17, turn.
Work as for 36-Stitch Short-Row Heel until 9 K sts rem after the slipped st.
HEEL TURN ROW 1: Sl 1, P8, Sl 1, pick up loop in the gap before the next st, P the Sl st and the loop together (HTR 1), turn.
HEEL TURN ROW 2: Sl 1, K8,
Sl 1, pick up and K 1 st in the gap before the next st, PSSO (HTR 2), turn.

Work as for 36-Stitch Short-Row Heel Turn until 16 K sts rem before HTR 2.

HEEL TURN ROW 11: Sl 1, P17, work as HTR 1, picking up the loop in the gap between the instep sts and heel sts, turn.

HEEL ROW 12: Sl 1, K9. New rnd begins in center of heel. Change yarn colors if instructed in individual pattern. Begin with new needle. K9, Sl 1, picking up the loop in the gap between the instep sts and heel sts, work as HTR 2. Redistribute sts on needles as desired.

18-Stitch Short-Row Heel

ROW 1: Sl 1, P16, turn.

ROW 2: Sl 1, K15, turn.

Work as for 36-Stitch Short-Row Heel until 7 K sts rem after the slipped st.

HEEL TURN ROW 1: Sl 1, P6, Sl 1, pick up loop in the gap before the next st, P the Sl st and the loop together (HTR 1), turn.

HEEL TURN ROW 2: Sl 1, K6, Sl 1, pick up and K1 st in the gap before the next st, PSSO (HTR 2), turn.

Work as for 36-Stitch Short-Row Heel Turn until 14 K sts rem before HTR 2.

HEEL TURN ROW 11: Sl 1, P16, work as HTR 1, picking up the loop in the gap between the instep and heel sts, turn.

HEEL TURN ROW 12: Sl 1, K8. New rnd begins in center of heel. Change yarn colors if instructed in individual pattern. Begin with new needle. K8, Sl 1, picking up the loop in the gap between the instep sts and heel sts, work as HTR 2. Redistribute sts on needles as desired.

STAR TOE DECREASES

A Star Toe decreases the foot stitches every other round, at even intervals (usually a multiple of six), generally beginning at the end of the little toe. The decreases form a clearly visible star-shaped design. The final 12 stitches are anchored by sewing yarn through the live loops, tightening and tying off, and weaving the yarn on the inside of the sock.

You work Star Toe toe-up socks in the same manner, by increasing the foot stitches every other round at even intervals, beginning with 12 stitches, and increasing until the proper number has been achieved for your desired sock size. Star Toe Increases also form a clearly visible star-shaped design at the end of the sock. You tighten the 12 cast-on stitches in much the same way that you tighten a Star Toe Decrease: by sewing through the cast-on loops, tightening, and tying off on the inside of the sock.

You can work nearly any sock with either a Wedge Toe or a Star Toe, as long as you take the difference in foot length into consideration and compensate by knitting ½ in. more (if you're converting from a Star Toe to a Wedge Toe) or ½ in. less (if you're converting from a Wedge Toe to a Star Toe) on the foot before beginning the decreases. You may need to decrease some of the foot stitches before beginning either toe decrease style.

72-Stitch Star Toe Decrease

DECREASE RND 1: *K10, K2 tog*, rep around. (66 sts rem)

Decrease Rnd 2 AND ALL EVEN TOE DECREASE RNDS UNTIL OTHERWISE NOTED: K.

DECREASE RND 3: *K9, K2 tog*, rep around. (60 sts rem)

DECREASE RND 5: *K8, K2 tog*, rep around. (54 sts rem)

DECREASE RND 7: *K7, K2 tog*, rep around. (48 sts rem)

DECREASE RND 9: *K6, K2 tog*, rep around. (42 sts rem)

DECREASE RND 11: *K5, K2 tog*, rep around. (36 sts rem)

DECREASE RND 13: *K4, K2 tog*, rep around. (30 sts rem)
DECREASE RND 15: *K3, K2 tog*, rep around. (24 sts rem)
DECREASE RND 17: *K2, K2 tog*, rep around. (18 sts rem)
DECREASE RND 18: *K1, K2 tog*, rep around. (12 sts rem). Cut a tail 12 in. long. Thread tail in a large-eye needle, and pull the needle through the remaining loops and tighten. Tie off on the inside of the sock.

66-Stitch Star Toe Decrease

Work as for 72-Stitch Star Toe Decrease, beginning at Rnd 3.
60-STITCH STAR TOE DECREASE: Work as for 72-Stitch Star Toe Decrease, beginning at Rnd 5.
54-STITCH STAR TOE DECREASE: Work as for 72-Stitch Star Toe Decrease, beginning at Rnd 7.
48-STITCH STAR TOE DECREASE: Work as for 72-Stitch Star Toe Decrease, beginning at Rnd 9.
42-STITCH STAR TOE DECREASE: Work as for 72-Stitch Star Toe Decrease, beginning at Rnd 11.
36-STITCH STAR TOE DECREASE: Work as for 72-Stitch Star Toe Decrease, beginning at Rnd 13.
30-STITCH STAR TOE DECREASE: Work as for 72-Stitch Star Toe Decrease, beginning at Rnd 15.
24-STITCH STAR TOE DECREASE: Work as for 72-Stitch Star Toe Decrease, beginning at Rnd 17.

WEDGE TOE DECREASES

You work a Wedge Toe by using stitch markers to mark the division between the sole and instep stitches, and then decreasing on either side of each marker. Four stitches are decreased every other round. When the desired number of stitches remains, you divide the stitches on two parallel needles, and close the opening using the Kitchener st.

You can work nearly any sock pattern with either a Wedge Toe or a Star Toe, as long as you take the difference in foot length into consideration and compensate by knitting ½ in. more (if you're converting from a Star Toe to a Wedge Toe) or ½ in. less (if you're converting from a Wedge Toe to a Star Toe) on the foot, before beginning the decreases.

Wedge Toe final stitch counts will vary depending on the weight of the yarn called for in the pattern and the size sock you are knitting.

Wedge Toe Decrease

On the last row or round before beginning the Wedge Toe Decreases, place the stitch markers as directed in your chosen pattern.
DECREASE RND 1: K to within 2 sts of marker, SSK, move marker, K2 tog, K to within 2 sts of marker, SSK, move marker, K2 tog, K to end. (4 sts dec)
DECREASE RND 2: K.
Rep Wedge Toe Decrease Rnds 1–2 until the proper number of sts rem (refer to individual patterns for the proper number of sts).
Knit to the next marker and arrange the sts, divided evenly on two needles. Use Kitchener st to close the toe opening. Weave all ends in on the inside of the sock.

Look for these other THREADS Selects booklets at www.taunton.com and wherever crafts are sold.

Baby Beanies
Debby Ware
EAN: 9781621137634
8 ½ x 10 ⅞, 32 pages
Product# 078001
$9.95 U.S., $11.95 Can.

Fair Isle Flower Garden
Kathleen Taylor
EAN: 9781621137702
8 ½ x 10 ⅞, 32 pages
Product# 078008
$9.95 U.S., $11.95 Can.

Fair Isle Hats, Scarves, Mittens & Gloves
Kathleen Taylor
EAN: 9781621137719
8 ½ x 10 ⅞, 32 pages
Product# 078009
$9.95 U.S., $11.95 Can.

Lace Socks
Kathleen Taylor
EAN: 9781621137894
8 ½ x 10 ⅞, 32 pages
Product# 078012
$9.95 U.S., $11.95 Can.

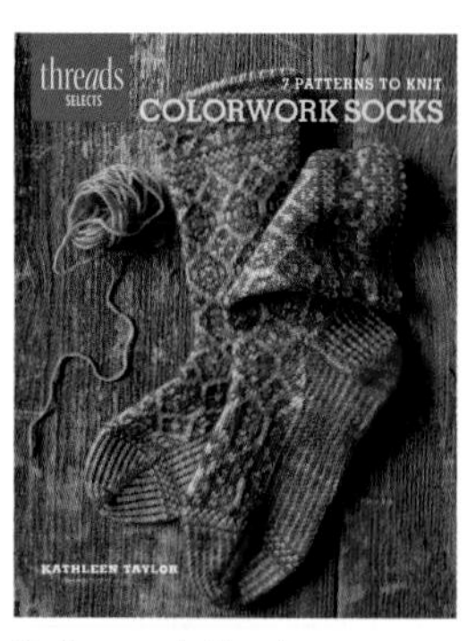

Colorwork Socks
Kathleen Taylor
EAN: 9781621137740
8 ½ x 10 ⅞, 32 pages
Product# 078011
$9.95 U.S., $11.95 Can.

DIY Bride Cakes & Sweets
Khris Cochran
EAN: 9781621137665
8 ½ x 10 ⅞, 32 pages
Product# 078004
$9.95 U.S., $11.95 Can.

DIY Bride Beautiful Bouquets
Khris Cochran
EAN: 9781621137672
8 ½ x 10 ⅞, 32 pages
Product# 078005
$9.95 U.S., $11.95 Can.

Bead Necklaces
Susan Beal
EAN: 9781621137641
8 ½ x 10 ⅞, 32 pages
Product# 078002
$9.95 U.S., $11.95 Can.

Drop Earrings
Susan Beal
EAN: 9781621137658
8 ½ x 10 ⅞, 32 pages
Product# 078003
$9.95 U.S., $11.95 Can.

Crochet Prayer Shawls
Janet Severi Bristow & Victoria A. Cole-Galo
EAN: 9781621137689
8 ½ x 10 ⅞, 32 pages
Product# 078006
$9.95 U.S., $11.95 Can.

Knitted Prayer Shawls
Janet Severi Bristow & Victoria A. Cole-Galo
EAN: 9781621137696
8 ½ x 10 ⅞, 32 pages
Product# 078007
$9.95 U.S., $11.95 Can.

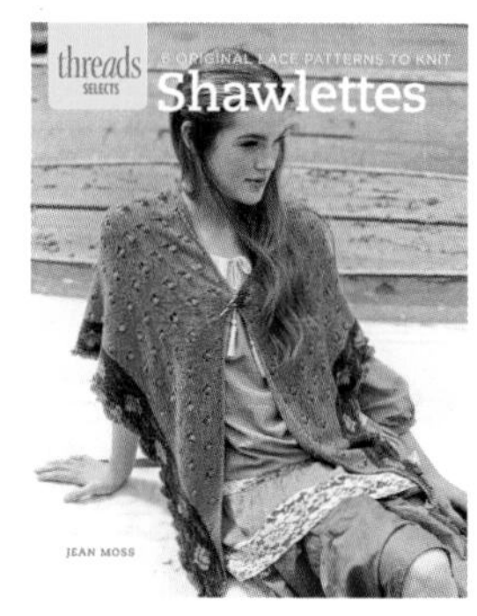

Shawlettes
Jean Moss
EAN: 9781621137726
8 ½ x 10 ⅞, 32 pages
Product# 078010
$9.95 U.S., $11.95 Can.